Lovers, Legends & Laments

A collection of 21 folk songs
from the British Isles arranged for
unaccompanied voices

SAT, SAA and SATB

Selected and arranged by

Sally J Davies

Illustrations by

Helen Lord

2nd Edition Jan 2017
First published in 2016 by Bonner Books

ISBN 978-1-5262-0542-1

Printed in Great Britain by
The Five Castles Press
Ipswich

FOREWORD

It is a privilege to write a few words as a foreword to this book of unique and beautiful arrangements.

I have been passionate about British and Irish traditional song since first being introduced to the genre in the early 1960s. However, there is a paradox in my writing this foreword, as, like most of the source/traditional singers of the lyric songs and ballads of these islands I have sung them solo and mostly unaccompanied over the intervening decades. I was lucky enough to work with both Bert Lloyd and Ewan MacColl and owe a great deal of my understanding to singer/scholar/collectors such as these.

With this experience and understanding, I nevertheless wholeheartedly endorse the arrangements Sally makes of these songs and the artistry and craft she uses to enhance and heighten both the music and words.

Although, like me, Sally loves the folk tradition of the UK she was also, as I was, introduced to the songs and strange, glorious harmonies of the Balkan and Georgian traditions. At first the dissonances of these harmonies can seem unsettling and even disturbing but the odd juxtaposition of sounds is arresting to the ear and stirs the emotions. They are often reminiscent of the harmonies of Early Music before the adoption of the major and minor scales came to dominate Western formal music. Sally's first great passion was for this Early Music and it was a fitting preparation for her later influences. And as the "folk" have always sung with the ancient modes which lend themselves to strange intervals and call forth evocative moods and imagery, it wasn't too big a leap for her to begin hearing these modal harmonies in British song.

It is also Sally's long involvement with Georgian singing both in London and Georgia as well as the huge attraction in the Community Choir movement to songs from the Balkans that honed Sally's ear to a different way of thinking about arranging British songs. Rather than using the 'cosier' harmonies often used for folk arrangements she looks to both the open harmonies of early music and these more dissonant musics for her inspiration. The very nature of her harmony creates a similar tension to the raw feeling of a single voice.

And her arrangements seem to me inspired; Sally brings all these influences to bear whilst maintaining a keen ear for the British Folk music traditions. This was brought home to me when I heard her version of a beautiful, moving song collected by Vaughan Williams called Lovely On the Water which was recorded by both Maddy Prior and myself. I would never have thought that I would feel happy to hear it arranged for 3 parts but when I did I found its haunting melody and its powerful words heightened. I was astonished; and since then both listening to Sally's arrangements and attending workshops run by her on harmonising I have found myself increasingly admiring and respectful of her artistry. I am sure you will be too and I wish you joy, excitement and "disturbance" taking these fine songs off the page and into the mouths of singers.

Frankie Armstrong

ARRANGER'S NOTE

All these arrangements were made to be learned by ear, as with folk songs the world over, even the polyphonic traditions. However, they are meant for all sorts of choirs and so, for those who learn from notation, they are laid out on the pages for ease of sight-reading. The contents of the book are arranged to some extent in order of difficulty, the songs towards the end of the collection being more challenging.

Unless otherwise indicated in the *Notes* on each song, most of these arrangements sound best sung in the octaves written i.e. not at an octave apart in any one harmony line. The tune is quite often with the men or the altos anyway (as indicated in the scores), and the harmony parts have a good tune of their own too, so from the point of view of having an interesting line to sing nobody need move. And, even if, occasionally, much of the part is a drone, (eg *Fine Flowers)* great musical satisfaction can be gained and much skill brought to bear on the steady holding of a harmonically vital drone note.

For quick reference, each song has its designated voice parts indicated on the contents page and at the top of each song eg SATB (Soprano, Alto, Tenor, Bass) etc. Where a song's parts are labelled 'SAB', the 'Bass' part is for tenor and bass singers together, although women tenors might choose to sing the alto line in these songs.

Nothing is set in stone however, and for textural variety, it can often be effective to leave out one or more of the harmony lines at your discretion for a certain verse; or for everyone to sing the tune in unison.

Very few directions about tempo or dynamics are included, leaving the singers or choir leader free to decide on these expressive elements. There are a few exceptions where the arranger felt some direction vital to the effectiveness of the scoring.

The majority of songs in this collection are (as far as we can know) English in origin. Many people when asked if they know a traditional English folk song will cite an Irish, Scottish or American one. Whatever the social and historical reasons for this, and wonderful as these traditions are, I have made this a predominantly English selection for the flourishing world of choirs and harmony singing as a contribution to these songs re-entering the collective ear, and so ensuring that their 'legendary' status is a living one.

Sally J Davies 2016

CD
Many of the song arrangements in this book are to be found on the *Cecil Sharp House Choir* CD *Twice Good Morning* which can be bought from the English Folk Dance and Song Society at http://www.cecilsharphouse.org/choir/recordings

SALLY J DAVIES

Sally Davies is a singer, composer, arranger, conductor, fiddle and baritone horn player. She is also the leader of the *Cecil Sharp House Choir* for which most of these songs were arranged. In 2008 Sally was asked by the *English Folk Dance and Song Society* (EFDSS) to direct a newly formed choir, which quickly grew to 70 members, has a constant waiting list and does many performances. Requests from other choir leaders for copies of her song arrangements have led to this publication.

Sally has worked with many choirs and singing groups and runs workshops all over the country and abroad teaching a mixture of these British folk song arrangements and the traditional polyphonic songs of Georgia and the Balkans.

With a background in theatre as a performer, composer and music director she continues to create music for theatre, most recently fulfilling commissions for the *Bath Literary Festival* and the *Bristol Festival of Ideas*. She also runs a choir in Hackney called *The Wing-It Singers* and she performs regularly with the duo *Bow and Bellows* and with the a capella group *4Folk*.

www.sallydaviesmusic.co.uk

Copyright and Acknowledgements

Unless otherwise stated, all songs are traditional with no known composer or lyricist. Exceptions to this:

Grace Darling Tune and lyrics by Felix McGlennon c 1880

Salley Gardens Lyrics by WB Yeats 1889

Jovial Broom Man Lyric by Richard Climsell 1640

Tom of Bedlam Tune by Nic Jones and Dave Moran in the 1960s. Published in "The Halliard: Broadside Songs" songbook. Copyright held by *Mollie Music*

Tommy Note Tune 'Structured' from traditional elements by Jon Raven in 1974

The Outlandish Knight Tune by Martin Carthy, registered by him as 'trad. *Arranged*, out there for all'

References

Recordings

England & Her Folk Songs EP. Collector Records (1962) AL Lloyd

Songs from the Sailing Barges. Topic LP (1978)

Lovely on the Water Topic LP Frankie Armstrong (1972)

Broadside Collections

Roxburghe Broadside collection. British Library

Theo Vasmer Broadside collection Birmingham Central Library

Books

Travellers Joy – Songs of the English and Scottish Gypsies published by EFDSS in 2006 (ISBN 0-85418-200-4)

A Little Book of Northamptonshire Songs compiled by Audrey Smith

John Playford's *The Dancing Master*, 4th edition, 1670.

The New Penguin Book of English Folk Songs, edited by Steve Roud and Julia Bishop 2012 (ISBN 978-0-141-19461-5)

Thanks

Special thanks to *Cecil Sharp House Choir* for their beautiful singing and their learning and enthusiasm in taking these songs off the page; to the *English Folk Dance and Song Society (EFDSS)* for setting up the choir, keeping the cogs running smoothly and being a superb repository of song material through the Vaughan Williams Memorial Library and online digital archive; to my Hackney choir *The Wing-It Singers,* who sing some of these arrangements interspersed with many inspiring songs from other lands; to the other members of my group, *4Folk*, Vivien Ellis, Dom Stichbury and Mikey Carlyon for proving that these song arrangements work as well for small groups as for large.

Other singers and scholars to whom I am very grateful:

Frankie Armstrong, Jean Ritchie, Venice Manley, Maddy Prior, Martin Carthy, Sam Lee, Carolyn Robson, Sarah Morgan, Nic Jones, Dave Moran, Pete Coe, Edisher Garakanidze, Dessislava Stefanova, Roy Palmer, Mike Yates, Steve Roud, Julian Elloway.

CONTENTS

For my father
Martin Bonner Davies
1919 - 2016

NOTES ON THE SONGS

1. **The False Knight upon the Road** (Roud 20, Child 3)
    Noted down by Cecil Sharp on a collecting trip to the Appalachians, this song, like many he found there, is a variant of an old British ballad. It features a riddling exchange between a schoolboy and the predatory devil in disguise. The boy stands fast; the devil cannot fool him. Such trickery is typical of folk tales and ballads from many European countries.
    Performance
    This antiphonal arrangement between men and women accentuates the drama. It is effective to start the last verse quiet and threatening and for the child's reply to crescendo through the line to a yell on 'hell!'

2. **Bushes and Briars** (Roud 1027)
    This is reputedly the song that kindled Ralph Vaughan Williams's interest in English folk music. He took it down from the singing of Charles Pottipher in the Essex village of Ingrave in the autumn of 1903. He commented that when he first heard it he felt the beautiful tune was one he had known all his life.
    Music notes
    As with the previous song the verse is unharmonised, while the chorus is in parts.

3. **The Oak and the Ash** (Roud 1367)
    The melody of this lament is printed as a dance tune in Playford's *The Dancing Master* of 1650, under the title 'Goddesses'. It may well have been a song before this time and is thought to be Northumbrian. The earliest printed version is in the Roxburgh collection.
    Performance
    You can choose in which of the verses you want the sopranos to sing the descant (and thus the altos to switch to the tune).
    Verse 3 (which is much less common than the other three verses) might be sung with more verve to contrast with the nostalgia.

4. **The Ballad of Grace Darling** (Roud 1441)
    Grace was a lighthouse keeper's daughter living on the Northumberland coast. She became famed the world over for participating in the rescue of nine survivors from a shipwreck in 1838. She died of tuberculosis four years later aged 26. This tune has more than a touch of the Music Hall about it and, written some time later in the 1880s by Felix McGlennon, is a highly romanticised version of events. Still, it's good to find a song where a woman doesn't have to dress up as a man to be brave.
    Performance
    The feel of the verses, which dramatically tell the story, is very different from the waltz-time chorus. The tempo of the verses can be pulled about while the chorus, by contrast, can be a rollicking um-pah-pah. Chord symbols are included for an accordion or a (preferably 'pub'-) piano.

5. **Down by the Salley Gardens**

   The Irish poet WB Yeats wrote the words of this song in 1889; he said himself that the poem was an attempt to reconstruct an old song from three lines, imperfectly remembered by an old peasant woman in the village of Ballisodare, Sligo. (The song was probably *You Rambling Boys of Pleasure*). Yeat's poem was set to music by Herbert Hughes in 1909 to the traditional air *The Moorlough Shore* (also known as *The Maids of Mourne Shore*). There is one theory that the Salley Gardens in Dublin are so called because of their willows. 'Salley' is an Anglicisation of the Irish *saileach*, meaning willow, i.e. a tree of the genus *Salix*.

   Music notes

   The tune (labelled in the score) switches between the soprano and alto parts.

6. **The London Wherryman**

   A wherry is a light rowing boat used for transporting people or goods on inland waterways. Bob Roberts, a skipper of sea-going barges on the Thames, can be heard singing this romantic song on the Topic LP *Songs from the Sailing Barges*. It was sung to me by the folk singer and song collector Sam Lee in 2009.

   Music notes

   The song is notated to be sung just by women at the octave written. But it could be sung with men distributed between the parts so that you have two octaves in each part. Or indeed transposed down for men in three parts.

7. **Broomdasher** (Roud 1733)

   There is a wonderful recording of Levi Smith singing this to Mike Yates in 1974. It is on the CD that accompanies the book *Travellers Joy – Songs of the English and Scottish Gypsies* published by EFDSS. The song is in Anglo-Romany and is about a poacher – a *broomdasher*.

   The words are also interesting from an ethnographic point of view because the idea that a naked thief is invisible is an echo of an old Indian belief.

   Performance

   Should be sung in a relaxed, conversational manner and with a bit of a swing. Suggested format: 1st time – unison; 2nd time – three-part harmony; 3rd time – with the cannon. The close-following cannon is a little tricky: everyone must feel the dotted crotchet pulse strongly then hold on to their hats and know when the end is coming!

8. **Woodford May Song** (Roud 21659)

   I happened upon this song on a YouTube clip of three unnamed people singing it in a pub. In a subsequent search I could only find it published in *A Little Book of Northamptonshire Songs* compiled by Audrey Smith.

   Performance

   In waltz time, it is quite possibly a song to dance to (in May) and sounds good with accordion accompaniment. Chord symbols included.

9. **Cuckoo in April** (Roud 413)

   Noted down by many collectors both in Britain and America, this particular tune was sung to George Butterworth in Sussex in 1909. However, it has many tunes and a whole variety of verses. The first three verses here are attributed to

Charlie Phillips of Symondsbury, Dorset and were collected by Peter
Kennedy. But the last verse, where the jilted girl refuses to go into a terminal
decline, is very similar to one sung by Jean Ritchie of Kentucky.
Music notes
The '*cuckoo*' introduction and refrain are the arranger's additions.

10. **Fine Flowers in the Valley** (Roud no. 9)
This is a Scottish variant of the ballad about infanticide often known as *The Cruel Mother*. This particular tune is notated in the above-mentioned book, *Travellers Joy – Songs of the English and Scottish Gypsies*. Compiled by Mike Yates, he comments that these bleak words are surprisingly often sung to the most beautiful tunes.
Performance
In truth, this arrangement probably sounds best and most eerie with one female voice per part. I have borrowed from the Bulgarian tradition of the accompanying voices singing a drone and a 'crooked drone' and the three parts are particularly close together in this song. So the song is labelled SAA. But it could be tried with mixed octaves in each part. It works well to rotate the three parts so that everyone has a chance to sing the tune. In this case, whoever sings the new harmony for verse 5 needs to be singing the tune for verse 6.

11. **Jovial Broom Man** (Roud V35538)
A man tells of his fantastical adventures at sea, although he quite possibly never left his seat in the corner of the pub. The song refers to the wars that took place abroad during the reign of Elizabeth I, though the text was actually written about 100 years later by Richard Climsell. It was set to an existing tune called 'Jamaica' or 'The Slow Men of London' which can be found in John Playford's *Dancing Master*, 4th edition, 1670.
Music notes
There are two different harmony arrangements. The melody is a good, rousing tune for men, and they have it for verses 1, 3 and 5. The sopranos have the tune in verses 2 and 4. The bass part, an octave under the tenor line, is optional.

12. **Lovely on the Water** (Roud 1539)
Another beautiful tune collected by Ralph Vaughan Williams from the singing of Mr Hilton at South Walsham a few miles from Norwich in 1908. This arrangement is inspired by both Frankie Armstrong and Maddie Prior's interpretations of the song

13. **The Press Gang** (Roud 601)
Cecil Sharp noted 29 songs from Jack Barnard (1863-1926) of Bridgwater between 1906-9, this being one of them. Unsurprisingly, songs about the press gang abound in the traditional repertoire of these islands, as do songs in which wealthy parents arrange for their daughter's poor suitor to be sent off to sea; this song ticks both boxes. It appeared on 19th-century broadside sheets, and versions have been collected all over the English-speaking world.
The number of songs about it would imply that over the centuries there must have been a fair number of women dressing up as men and passing themselves

off as sailors in order to follow their true loves to sea. A tricky business, not least because if discovered, they risked being thrown overboard. This song has a happier outcome.

14. **Barbara Ellen** (Roud 54)
In *The New Penguin Book of English Folk Songs*, Steve Roud comments that Barbara Allen (or Ellen) is 'far away the most widely collected song in the English language – equally popular in England, Scotland and Ireland with hundreds of tunes collected over the years'. This tune was collected from William Pittaway by Cecil Sharp, May 1923, at Burford, Oxfordshire. Notated in 5/4, it is by no means the only one with an uneven metre.
Performance
The dialogue can be picked out by the men singing the lyrics for Edwin, while the other parts hum or 'oo' and vice versa for Barbara's words.

15. **Lovely Joan** (Roud 592)
Ralph Vaughan Williams collected *Lovely Joan* in a Norfolk pub from a labourer named Christopher Jay in 1908. At first, the words were only published in a modified form by RVW's publishers on account of the lyrics being thought immodest and too anatomically specific.
Music notes
It seems apt for this song to be sung by women only. But though it is scored for three women's voices, Alto 2 can be sung an octave lower by men. Alternatively, mix men and women (an octave apart) on each line.

16. **The Dear Companion** (Roud 411)
Sung to Cecil Sharp by Rosie Hensley, North Carolina, this is a version of the song *Go and Leave Me If You Wish It*, which has been found all over Britain. Cecil Sharp was fascinated to find British songs that had migrated over the Atlantic and although it may have been a romantic notion he believed they had been preserved in the Appalachian Mountains in an 'earlier' form.
Performance
Although notated in three-part harmony, it is also very poignant to have the first verse of this sad song sung solo by a woman.

17. **The Misery of the Framework Knitters** (Roud V20853)
This is a kind of Luddite propaganda song from Nottinghamshire. It was published as a Broadside sheet in1811. Factory knitting machines posed a huge threat to the domestic knitting industry and raiding parties would go out to smash up these new big machines. In this song they are appealing to the listeners to understand their point of view.
Bag Masters – middle-men who sold the knitted goods for the framework knitters and often paid them in a currency only redeemable in the boss's shop.
Bowl in – smash up.

18. **Poverty Knock** (Roud 3491)
One of many songs chronicling the awful conditions the factory workers had to endure in the cloth mills around 1900. The clatter of the old Dobbie loom sounded as if it was constantly saying 'Poverty knock!' Apparently, it was so noisy in the factory that everyone learned to lip-read. AE Green recorded this

song in 1965 from an elderly weaver of Batley, Tom Daniel, who said he remembered hearing it in his youth. This is a minor key version of the song from the singing of Pete Coe.

19. **Tom of Bedlam** (Roud V16366)

The first written record of this song, as a poem, dates from 1618 and it is one of the oldest known songs or poems about madness. Bedlam was a common name for St Mary Bethlehem hospital in London that housed 'the insane'. During the 18th century it was a popular diversion to visit the hospital (who charged a penny entrance fee) to watch the antics of the poor inmates. The words have been set to several tunes over the centuries, but this one was written by Nic Jones and Dave Moran in the 1960s.

Music notes

Here is a useful plan of the arrangement:

Verses 1, 3 and 8 are the same harmonically for everybody

Verses 2 and 4 are the same as each other

Verses 5 and 6 are the same as each other

Verse 7, everyone sings the tune in unison

The chorus is first of all sung just to a drone accompaniment and thereafter either the 'harmony' version or the 'cannon' version as indicated.

After verse 4 there is no introduction of *Bedlam mad Bedlam* again until verse 8.

20. **Tommy Note**

The text was printed as a broadside by T Bloomer of Birmingham around the middle of the 19th century and can be found in broadside collections of both Theo Vasmer and Cecil Sharp (though this version is somewhat shortened). This melody was structured from traditional elements by Jon Raven in 1974. The Tommy Shop was the truck shop owned by the employers, where food and other goods were of inferior quality and superior prices. Until the Truck Acts stopped this practice, the canal folk were often paid in full or part by 'tommy notes' which could only be redeemed at the company store.

21. **Outlandish Knight** (Roud 21, Child 4)

'Outlandish' here means coming from beyond the northern border – that is, Scotland.

It tells the story of a beguiling lover who entices a whole sequence of girls to their deaths but gets his come-uppance. There are a great many variants from all over Europe, with many tunes, but this is a comparatively recent one from the singing of Martin Carthy.

Music notes

Appreciation for this arrangement from members of the Cecil Sharp House Choir, for whom it was written, include 'It's a whole folk-opera in one song!' It is another arrangement where the dialogue (and therefore the vocal accompaniment) switches between the women's and men's voices. Verse 11 where she hurls him into the sea is arguably the most 'operatic'.

SJD 2016

The False Knight upon the Road

SAB

Last chorus: for a dramatic ending you can do this for the last line of the song

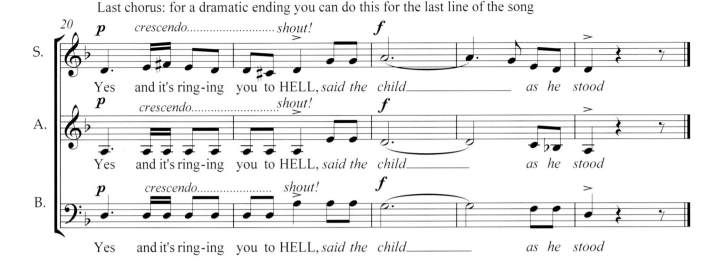

S. Yes   and it's ring-ing you to HELL, *said the child_____ as he stood*

A. Yes   and it's ring-ing you to HELL, *said the child_____ as he stood*

B. Yes   and it's ring-ing you to HELL, *said the child_____ as he stood*

INTRO. The knight met a child in the road.

1. O where are you going to? *said the knight in the road*
I'm a-going to my school, *said the child as he stood*
Chorus
He stood and he stood and it's well because he stood
I'm a-going to my school *said the child as he stood*

2. O what are you going there for? *said the knight in the road*
For to learn the word of God, *said the child as he stood*
Chorus
He stood and he stood and it's well because he stood
For to learn the word of God *said the child as he stood*

3. O what have you got there? *said the knight in the road*
I have got my bread and cheese, *said the child as he stood*
Chorus

4. O won't you give me some? *said the knight in the road*
No, ne're a bite nor crumb, *said the child as he stood*
Chorus

5. I wish you was on the sands, s*aid the knight in the road*
Yes and a good staff in my hands, *said the child as he stood*
Chorus

6. I wish you was in the sea, s*aid the knight in the road*
Yes and a good boat under me, *said the child as he stood*
Chorus

7. I think I hear a bell, s*aid the knight in the road*
Yes and it's ringing you to hell, *said the child as he stood*
Chorus

Bushes and Briars

SATB

Traditional
arr. Sally J Davies

Men (or male soloist) *first four verses*

1. Through bushes and through briars I lately took my way
   All for to hear the small birds sing and the lambs to skip and play
Chor: (All) *All for to hear the small birds sing and the lambs to skip and play*

2. I overheard my own true love, her voice it was so clear
   Long time I have been waiting for the coming of my dear
Chor: *Long time I have been waiting for the coming of my dear*

3. I drew myself unto a tree, a tree that did look green
   Where the leaves shaded over us we scarcely could be seen
Chor: *Where the leaves shaded over us we scarcely could be seen*

4. I sat myself down by my love as she began to mourn
   I'm of this opinion that my heart is not my own
Chor: *I'm of this opinion that my heart is not my own*

Women (or female soloist) *till end*
5. Sometimes I am uneasy and troubled in my mind
   Sometimes I think I'll go to my love and tell to him my mind
Chor: (All) Sometimes I think I'll go to my love and tell to him my mind

6. And if I should go to my love, my love he will say nay
   If I show to him my boldness, he'd ne'er love me again
Chor: If I show to him my boldness, he'd ne'er love me again

7. I cannot think the reason young women love young men
   For they are so false hearted young women to trepan**
Chor: For they are so false hearted young women to trepan**

8. For they are so false hearted young women to trepan,
   So the green grave shall see me, for I can't love that man
Chor: So the green grave shall see me, for I can't love that man

**[Trepan (archaic) - to trap; ensnare.]

The Oak and the Ash

Traditional
arr. Sally J Davies

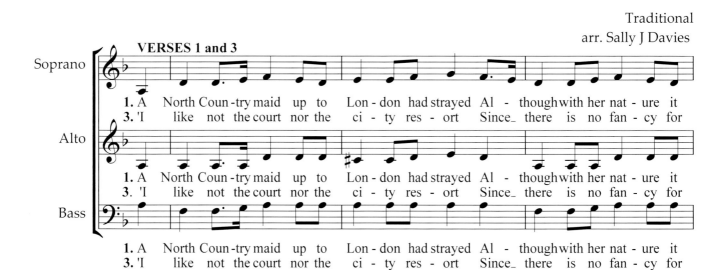

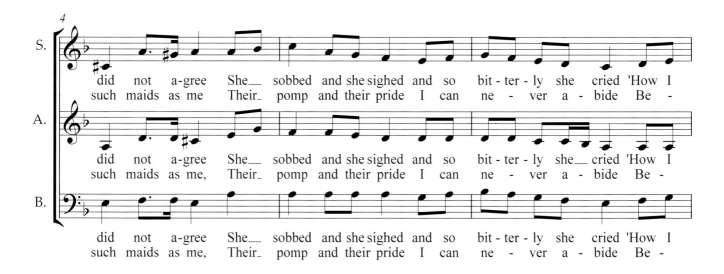

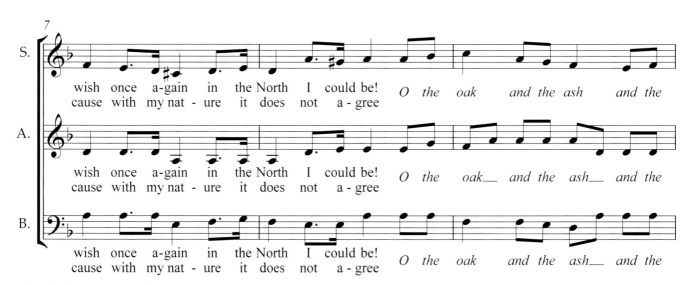

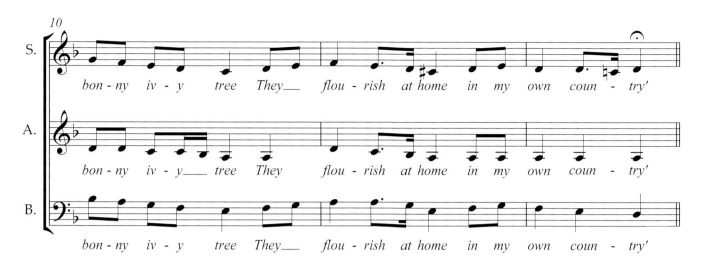

bon - ny iv - y tree They___ flou - rish at home in my own coun - try'

bon - ny iv - y___ tree They flou - rish at home in my own coun - try'

bon - ny iv - y tree They___ flou - rish at home in my own coun - try'

VERSES 2 and 4

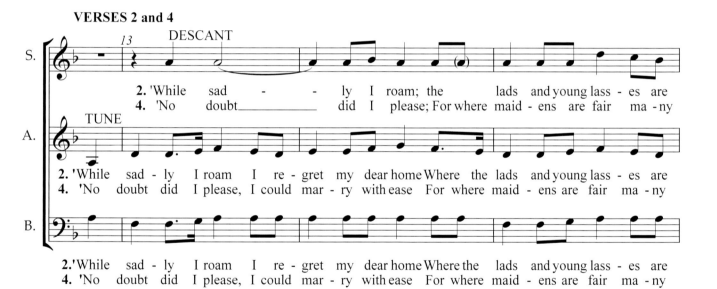

DESCANT

2. 'While sad - - ly I roam; the lads and young lass - es are
4. 'No doubt_____ did I please; For where maid - ens are fair ma - ny

TUNE

2. 'While sad - ly I roam I re - gret my dear home Where the lads and young lass - es are
4. 'No doubt did I please, I could mar - ry with ease For where maid - ens are fair ma - ny

2.'While sad - ly I roam I re - gret my dear home Where the lads and young lass - es are
4. 'No doubt did I please, I could mar - ry with ease For where maid - ens are fair ma - ny

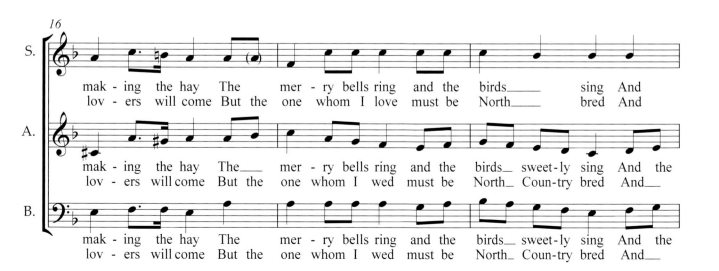

mak - ing the hay The mer - ry bells ring and the birds___ sing And
lov - ers will come But the one whom I love must be North___ bred And

mak - ing the hay The___ mer - ry bells ring and the birds_ sweet-ly sing And the
lov - ers will come But the one whom I wed must be North_ Coun-try bred And_

mak - ing the hay The mer - ry bells ring and the birds_ sweet-ly sing And the
lov - ers will come But the one whom I wed must be North_ Coun-try bred And_

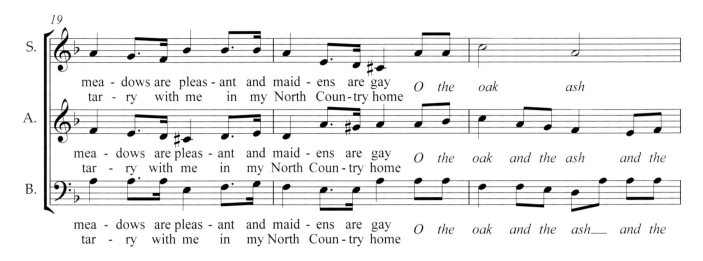

1. A North Country maid up to London had strayed
Although with her nature it did not agree
She sobbed and she sighed and so bitterly she cried
'How I wish once again in the North I could be!
Chorus: O the oak and the ash and the bonny ivy tree
They flourish at home in my own country'

2. 'While sadly I roam I regret my dear home
Where the lads and young lasses are making the hay
The merry bells ring and the birds sweetly sing
And the meadows are pleasant and maidens are gay
Chorus: O the oak and the ash..........

3. 'I like not the court, nor the city resort
Since there is no fancy for such maids as me
Their pomp and their pride I can never abide
Because with my humour it does not agree
Chorus: O the oak and the ash............

4. 'No doubt did I please, I could marry with ease
For where maidens are fair many lovers will come
But the one whom I wed must be North Country bred
And tarry with me in my North Country home
Chorus: O the oak and the ash............

The Ballad of Grace Darling

SAB

with Accordion/piano chords

Dramatic Music Hall style
(Verses could be sung solo or by a trio.)

Felix McGlennon c. 1880
arr. Sally J Davies

Soprano / Alto / Bass:
Twas on the Long-stone light house there dwelt an Eng-lish maid Pure as the air a-round her of dan-ger ne'er a-fraid One morn-ing just at day-break a storm-tossed wreck she spied Then up spake brave Grace Dar-ling "I'll save the crew" she cried

CHORUS almost twice as fast; waltz time

So she pulled a-way on the rol-ling sea Ov-er the wat-ers blue_____ "Help

1. 'Twas on the Longstone lighthouse
there dwelt an English maid
Pure as the air around her
of danger ne'er afraid
One morning just at daybreaks
a storm-tossed wreck she spied
And up spake brave Grace Darling
"I'll save the crew" she cried

Chorus

So she pulled away on the rolling sea
over the waters blue
"Help, help!" she could hear the cry
of the shipwrecked crew
But Grace had an English heart
and the raging storm she braved
She pulled away o'er the rolling sea
and the crew she saved

2. They to the rock were clinging
a crew of nine all told.
Between them and the lighthouse
the seas like mountains rose.
Said Grace "Come help me father,
we'll launch the boat," said she.
Her father cried "'Tis madness,
to face that raging sea"
Chorus
But she pulled away on the rolling sea

3. One murmured prayer "heaven guard us"
and then they were afloat
Between them and destruction
the planks of that frail boat.
Then spoke the maiden's father
"Return or doomed are we"
But up spoke brave Grace Darling
"Alone I'll brave the sea"
Chorus:
So she pulled away......

4. They bravely rode the billows
and reached the rock at length
They saved the storm-tossed sailors
in heaven alone their strength
Oh tell the wide world over
what English pluck can do
And sing of brave Grace Darling
who nobly saved the crew
Chorus:
When she pulled away......

Down by the Salley Gardens

SAB

Poem - WB Yeats
Tune - Traditional
arr. Sally J Davies

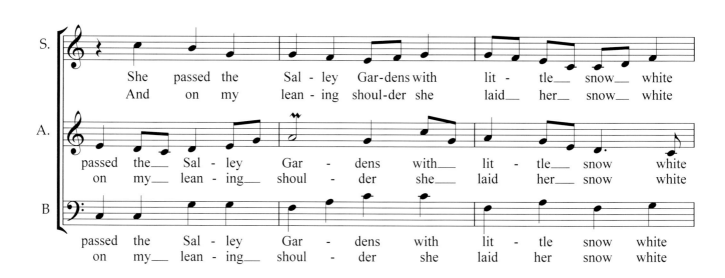

1. Down by the Salley Gardens my love and I did meet
She passed the Salley Gardens with little snow white feet
She bade me take love easy as the leaves grow on the tree
But I being young and foolish with her did not agree

2. In a field down by the river my love and I did stand
And on my leaning shoulder she laid her snow white hand
She bade me take life easy as the grass grows on the weir
But I was young and foolish and now am full of tears

The London Wherryman

SAA

Traditional
arr. Sally J Davies

A. he be-came known as the young lov-ers' fer-ry but he could not find a true love of his_ own

A.1 he be-came known as the young lov-ers' fer-ry but he could not find a true love of his own

A.2 he be-came known as the young lov-ers' fer-ry but he could not find a true love of his own

1. Have you ever heard tell of a young London waterman
who from Blackfriars did regular ply?
And he feathered his oars with such skill and dexterity
pleasing each maid and delighting each eye
And he sang so sweet he sang so merry
the couples all jostled to hire his wherry
And he became known as the young lovers' ferry
but he could not find a true love of his own

2. Till there came a young goose girl from Stratford St Mary
and she wanted taking to Farringdon Fair
But she had not the ha'penny to pay for her wherry
and stood on the steps in a pretty despair
But she sang so sweet she sang so merry
he put her and all of her geese in his wherry
And her pretty face was a far farer ferry
and rode her across to Farringdon fair

3. They were married next May time at Stratford St Mary
and now they have watermen one two three four
And they feather their oars with such skill and dexterity
rowing the people from shore to shore
And they sing so sweet they sing so merry
the couples all jostle to hire their wherry
And everyone goes by the Blackfriars ferry
while he stays at home with a love of his own

The Broomdasher

SAB

Traditional
arr. Sally J Davies

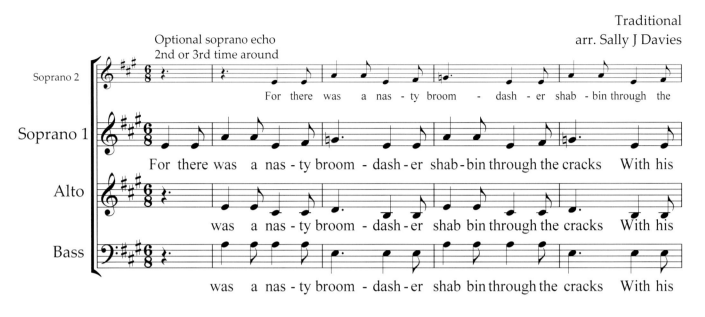

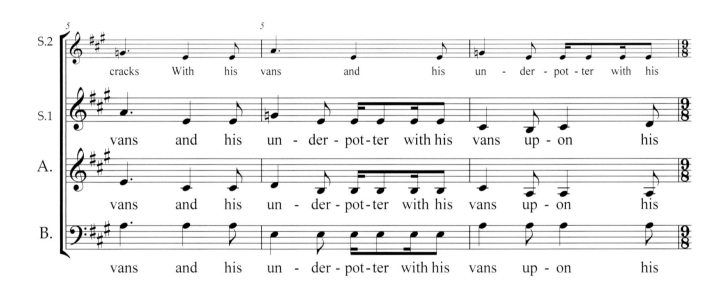

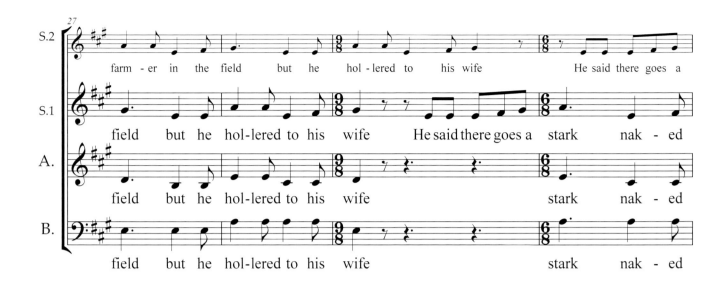

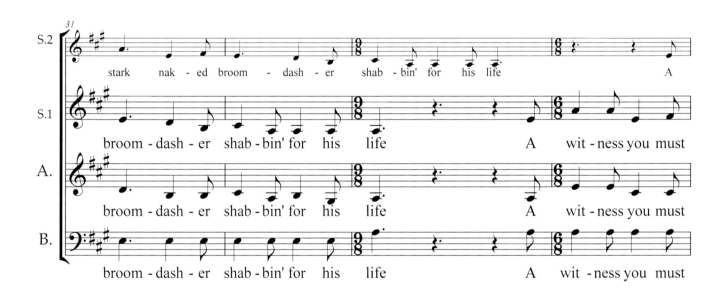

The Broomdasher

For there was a nasty broomdasher
shabbin' through the cracks
With his vans and his underpotter
with his vans upon his back
For he met with the yogger
for he stamped and he swore
You can believe me Mister Yogger
I've never been here before
As the broomdasher rises up on his feet
he did pogger him nice and neat
And away goes the broomdasher shabbin for his life
He said there was a farmer in the field
but he hollered to his wife
He said there goes a stark naked broomdasher
shabbin' for his life
A witness you must be
but No says the farmer
Its nothing to do with me

***Romany to* English**
broomdasher = poacher
shabbin' = running
cracks = fields
yogger = gamekepper
pogger = hit

Woodford May Song

SATB
with optional accordion accompaniment chords

Traditional
arr. Sally J Davies

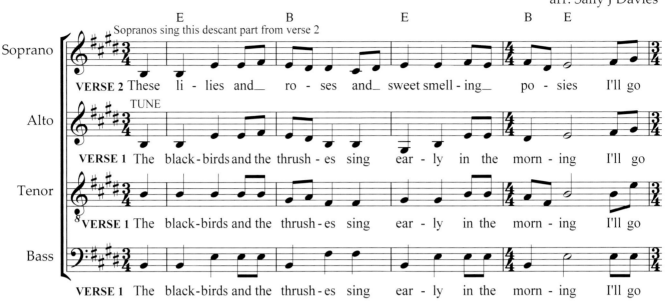

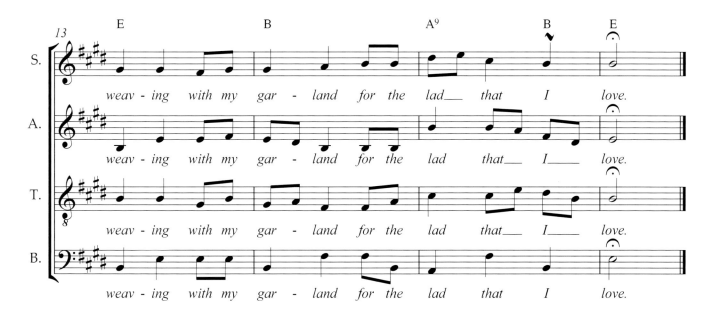

1. The blackbirds and the thrushes sing early in the morning
I'll go weaving with my garland for the lad that I love
Chor: *For the lad that I love for the lad that I love*
I'll go weaving with my garland for the lad that I love

2. These lilies and roses and sweet smelling posies
I'll go weaving with my garland for the lad that I love
Chor: For the lad that I love etc.

3. Here's cowslips and posies and sweet smelling primroses
I'll go weaving with my garland for the lad that I love
Chor: For the lad that I love etc.

4. Here's bobbins and spangles hang over these bowers
I'll go weaving with my garland for the lad that I love
Chor: For the lad that I love etc.

Reprise
For the lad that I love for the lad that I love
I'll go weaving with my garland for the lad that I love

Cuckoo in April

SATB

Traditional
arr. Sally J Davies

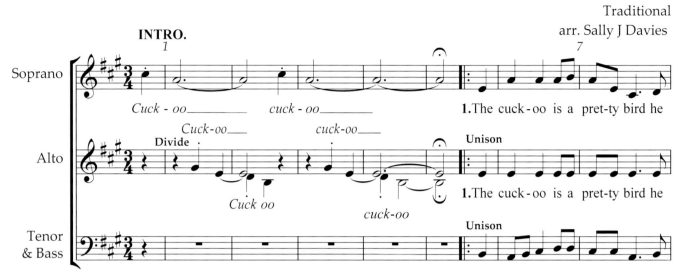

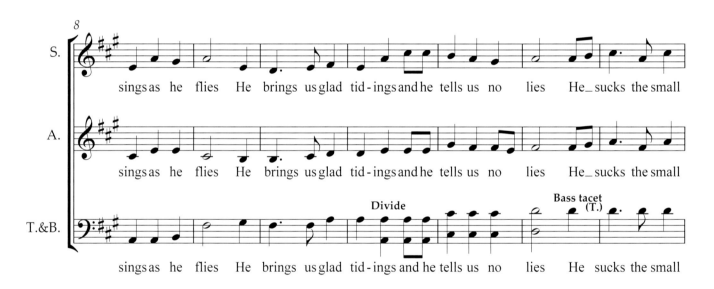

INTRO: *Cuckoo cuckoo cuckoo (X2)*

1. The cuckoo is a pretty bird he sings as he flies
He brings us glad tidings and he tells us no lies
He sucks the small birds' eggs to keep his voice clear
And he sings to us sweetly three months of the year
Cuckoo cuckoo cuckoo (X2)
Chorus
Cuckoo in April, cuckoo in May,
Cuckoo in June and July fly away.

2. A-walking and a-talking and a-walking went I
To meet my true lover, he'll be here by and by
To meet him in the meadow it is my delight
Then we'll go a-walking from morning till night
Cuckoo cuckoo cuckoo (X2)
Chorus
Cuckoo in April etc.

3. Oh meeting is a pleasure and parting is a grief
And a false hearted lover's far worse than a thief
A thief will but rob you and take all you've saved
But an inconstant lover will turn you to the grave
Cuckoo cuckoo cuckoo (X2)
Chorus
Cuckoo in April etc.

4. Although he forswears me, I'll not be forsworn,
And though he forsakes me, I'll not be forlorn
But I'll get myself up in my best finery
And I'll walk as proud by him as he walks by me
Cuckoo cuckoo cuckoo (X2)
Chorus
Cuckoo in April etc.

Fine Flowers in the Valley

(The Cruel Mother)
SAA or TBB

Traditional
arr. Sally J Davies

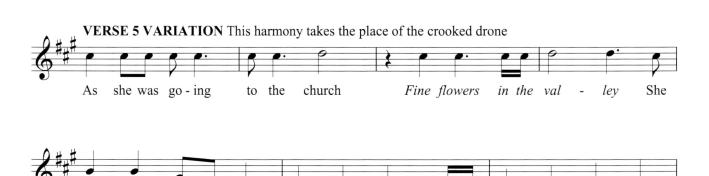

Fine Flowers in the Valley

1. She sat down below a thorn
Fine flowers in the valley
And there she has her babe new born
And the green leaves they grow rarely

2. Smile not so sweet, my bonnie babe
Fine flowers in the valley
And you smile so sweet, you will smile me dead
And the green leaves they grow rarely

3. She's taken out her little penknife
Fine flowers in the valley
And robbed the sweet babe of its life,
And the green leaves they grow rarely

4. She has dug a grave by the light of the moon,
Fine flowers in the valley
And there she has laid her sweet babe in,
And the green leaves they grow rarely

5. As she was going to the church,
Fine flowers in the valley
She saw a sweet babe in the porch,
And the green leaves they grow rarely

6. O sweet babe and you were mine
Fine flowers in the valley
I would clothe you in the silk so fine
And the green leaves they grow rarely

7. O mother dear, when I was thine
Fine flowers in the valley
You did not prove to me so kind
And the green leaves they grow rarely

The Jovial Broom Man

SATB

Traditional
arr. Sally J Davies

The Jovial Broom Man

1. Make room for a man that's come from seas
Hey the jolly broom man
That gladly now would take his ease
And therefore make thee room man
To France the Netherlands and Spain
Hey the jolly broom man
I crossed the seas and back again
And therefore make thee room man

2. Yet in these countries there lived I
Hey the jolly broom man
And valiant soldiers I've seen die
And therefore make thee room man
Ten thousand gallants there I killed
Hey the jolly broom man
Besides a sea of blood I spilt
And therefore make thee room man

3. In Germany I took a town
Hey the jolly broom man
And threw the walls there upside down
And therefore make thee room man
In Tilbury camp with Captain Drake
Hey the jolly broom man
I caused the Spanish fleet to quake
And therefore make thee room man

3. In Holland leaguer there I fought
Hey the jolly broom man
But there the service proved too hot
And therefore make thee room man
So from the siege returned I
Hey the jolly broom man
Naked, hungry, cold and dry
And therefore make thee room man

4. So now I have compassed the globe
Hey the jolly broom man
And I returned as poor as Job
And therefore make thee room man
So now I'm safe returned here
Hey the jolly broom man
Just bring me a cup of English beer
And therefore make thee room man

Lovely on the Water

SAB

Traditional
arr. Sally J Davies

As__ I walked out one__ morn- ing In the spring-time of the year_____ I

o - ver heard a young sai - lor Like - wise his la - dy fair

VERSE 2

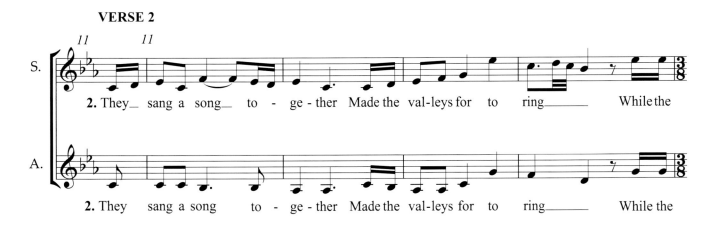

2. They__ sang a song__ to - ge - ther Made the val-leys for to ring_____ While the

2. They sang a song to - ge - ther Made the val-leys for to ring_____ While the

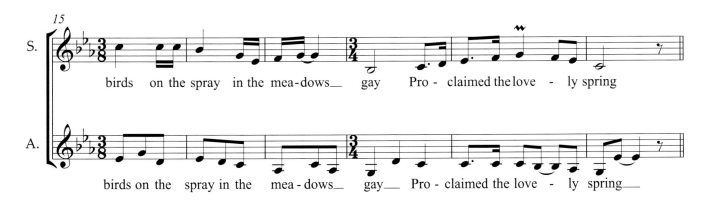

birds on the spray in the mea-dows__ gay Pro - claimed the love - ly spring

birds on the spray in the mea - dows__ gay__ Pro - claimed the love - ly spring__

VERSES 3 and 5

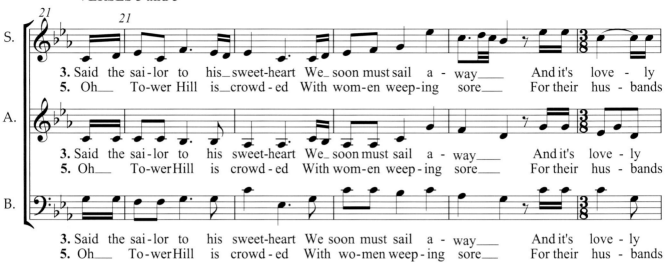

3. Said the sai-lor to his sweet-heart We soon must sail a - way___ And it's love - ly
5. Oh___ To-wer Hill is crowd - ed With wom-en weep-ing sore___ For their hus - bands

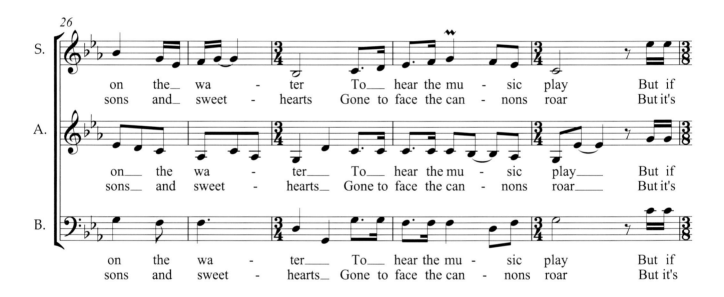

on the wa - ter To___ hear the mu - sic play But if
sons and sweet - hearts Gone to face the can - nons roar But it's

I had my way my___ dear-est love A - long with you___ I'd stay
love - ly on the___ wa - ter To___ hear the mu - sic play

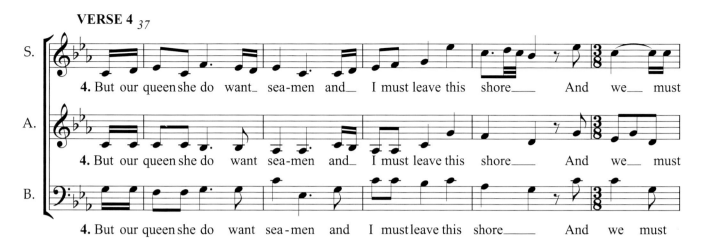

1. As I walked out one morning
In the springtime of the year
I overheard a young sailor
Likewise his lady fair

2. They sang a song together,
Made the valleys for to ring
While the birds on the spray in the meadows gay
Proclaimed the lovely spring.

3. Said the sailor to his sweetheart
We soon must sail away
And it's lovely on the water
To hear the music play
But if I had my way my dearest love
Along with you I'd stay

4. But our Queen she do want seamen
And we must leave this shore
And we must face the wars, my love
Where the blund'ring cannons do roar

5. Oh Tower Hill is crowded
With women weeping sore
For their husbands, sons and sweethearts
Gone to face the cannons roar
But it's lovely on the water
To hear the music play

The Press Gang
SATB

Traditional
arr. Sally J Davies

The Press Gang

1. It's of a rich gentleman in London did dwell
He had but one daughter, most beautiful girl
Three squires came a-courting but she refused all
'I will marry a sailor that's proper and tall

2. Now father, dear father, now hinder me not
I'll marry a sailor it will be my lot
To see him in his charm with a smile on his face
I'm sure that a sailor he is no disgrace'

3. They walked out and they talkéd both night and day
They walked and they talked and fixed the wedding day
The old man overheard it and this he did say
'He shan't marry my daughter, I'll press him to sea'

4. As they was a-walking up to the church door
The press gang o'ertook him and from her him tore
They pressed this young fellow all on the salt sea
Instead of getting married he sorrowed for she

5. So she cut off her hair and she altered her clothes
And to the press master she immediately goes
Saying 'Press master, press master, do you want a man?
I am willing and ready to do what I can.'

6. Then she shipped on board 'twas that very same day
And her true love she found but no word did she say
True love for a messmate, you quickly shall hear
She did sleep by his side for a full half a year

7. Now one morning, one morning as these two arose
They got into discourse as they put on their clothes
He said, 'Once I had a sweetheart, in London dwelt she
But it's her cruel father that's pressed me to sea'

8. She went up close to him, 'Now look well on me
Beneath this man's clothing your sweetheart you'll see
Oh let us be married before our ship's crew
We won't care for my father nor all he can do'

Barbara Ellen

SAA/TB

Traditional
arr. Sally J Davies

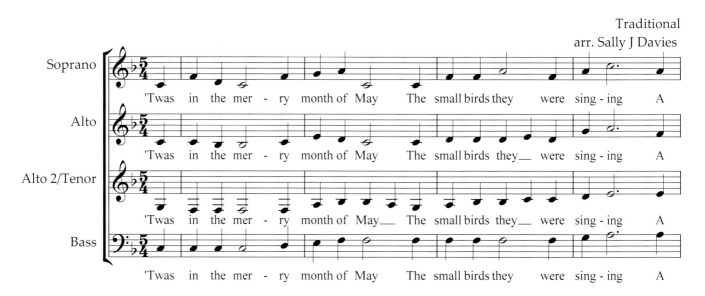

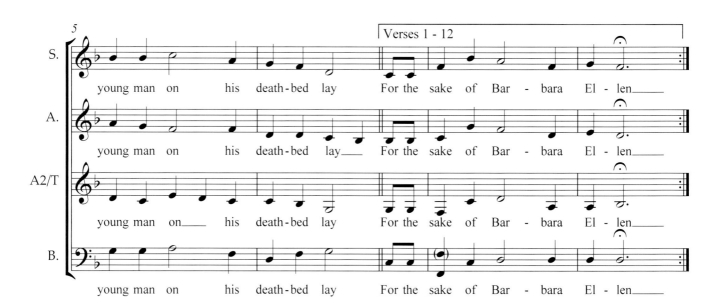

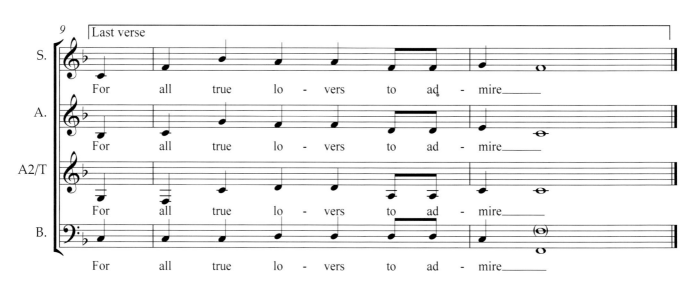

Barbara Ellen

1. 'Twas in the merry month of May
The small birds they were singing
A young man on his death-bed lay
For the sake of Barbara Ellen

2. He sent one of his servants down
To the house where she was dwelling,
Saying 'You must come to my master,
If your name is Barbara Ellen'
.
3. So slowly she put on her clothes,
And slowly she came to him,
And when she came to his bedside,
Says she 'Young man you're dying'

4. 'I'm not a-dying now just yet
One kiss of thine will cure me'
'One kiss of mine you never shall have
So fare away, young Edwin'

5. 'Now you look over my bedside,
You'll see my waistcoat hanging
With my gold watch and silver chain.
Give these to Barbara Ellen'

6. So she looked over his bedside
And saw the waistcoat hanging.
'That shall be mine for I won't be thine,
So fare away, young Edwin'

7. 'Now you look out to the raging sea
You'll see my five ships sailing
They shall be yours if you'll be mine
For I love you Barbara Ellen'

8. So she looked out to the raging sea
And saw those five ships sailing
'They shan't be mine for I won't be thine
So fare away young Edwin'

9. As she was a-walking up the street
She saw the corpse a-coming.
She cried 'Put him down a little while
That I might gaze upon him'

10. The more she gazed the more she smiled
And the nearer she came to him
Until her friends cryed out 'For shame:
Hard-hearted Barbara Ellen'

11. 'O Mother Mother make my bed
O make it long and narrow
Since my love died for me today
I'll die for him tomorrow'

12. Now he was buried in the tomb
And the other in the church.
And out of him there sprang a rose
And growed from her sweetbriar
.
13. It growed and growed till it reached the top
And it could grow no higher
They tied it in a true-love's knot
For all true lovers to admire

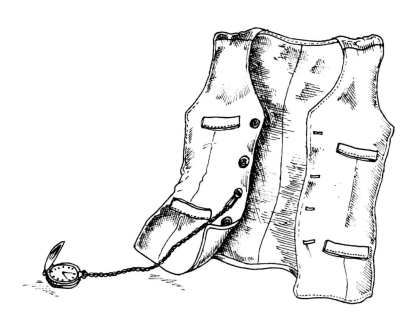

Lovely Joan

SAA

Traditional
arr. Sally J Davies

VERSES 3 to 7
Suggestion: For variety leave out Alto 2 for verse 5

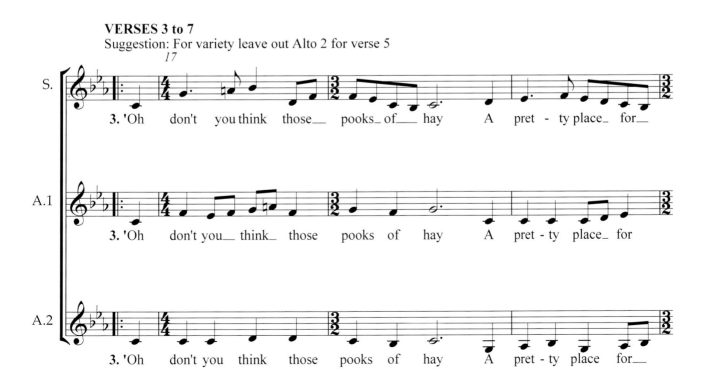

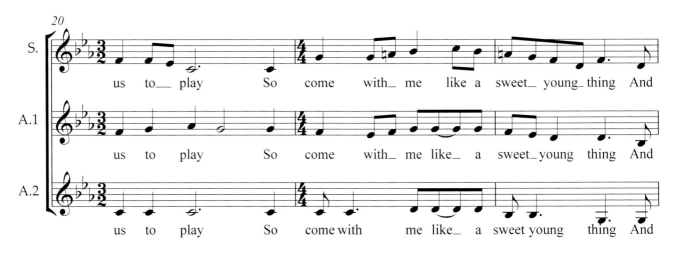

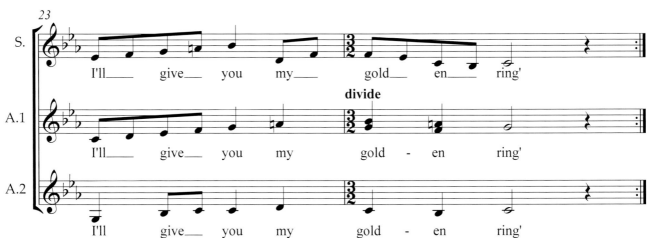

1. A fine young man it was indeed
Was mounted on his milk white steed
He rode and he rode himself all alone
Until he came to lovely Joan

2 'Good morning to you, pretty maid'
'And twice good morning, sir,' she said
He gave her a wink she rolled her eye
Says he to himself 'I'll be there by and by'

3. 'Oh don't you think those pooks of hay
A pretty place for us to play?
So come with me like a sweet young thing
And I'll give you my golden ring'

4. Then he pulled off his ring of gold
'My pretty little miss do this behold.
I'd freely give it for your maidenhead,'
And her cheeks they blushed like the roses red

5. 'Give me that ring into my hand
And I will neither stay nor stand
For this would do more good to me
Than twenty maidenheads' said she.

6. And as he made for the pooks of hay
She leapt on his horse and tore away.
He called, he called but twas all in vain
Young Joan she never looked back again.

7. She didn't think herself quite safe
No not till she came to her true love's gate
She's robbed him of his horse and ring
And left him to rage in the meadows green

The Dear Companion

SATB

Traditional
arr. Sally J Davies

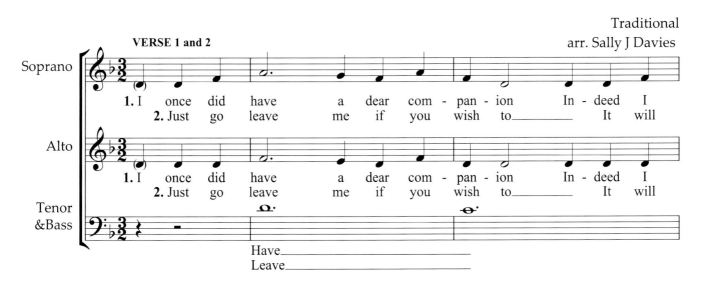

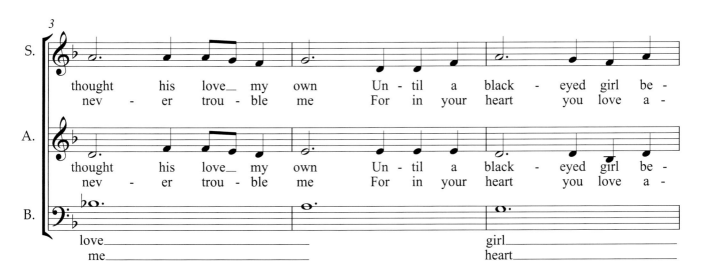

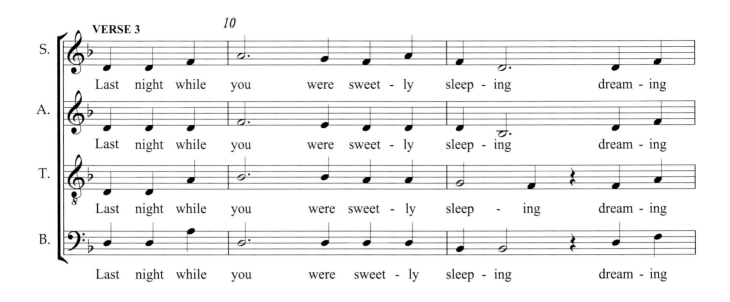

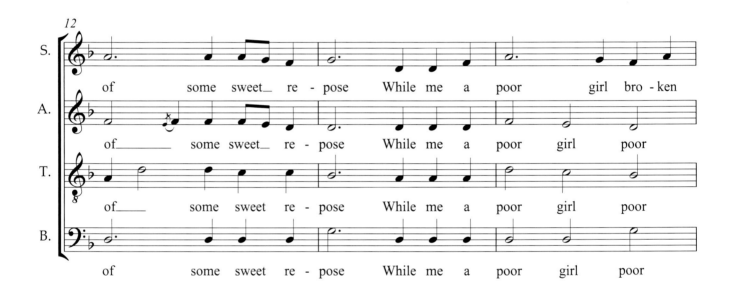

1. I once did have a dear companion
Indeed I thought his love my own
Until a black-eyed girl betrayed me
And then he cared no more for me

2. Just go leave me if you wish to
It will never trouble me
For in your heart you love another
And in my grave I'd rather be

3. Last night while you where sweetly sleeping
Dreaming of some sweet repose
While me a poor girl broken hearted
Listen to the wind that blows

4. When I see your babe a-laughing
It makes me think of your sweet face
But when I see your babe a-crying
It makes me think of my disgrace

The Miseries of the Framework Knitters

SATB

Tune Traditional
arr. Sally J Davies

The Miseries of the Framework Knitters

1.Ye kind hearted souls pray attend to our song
And hear the true story it shall not be long
Framework knitters of Sutton how ill we are used
And by the bag masters so sorely abused
Chorus: *Derry down down hey derry down*

2. They've bated the wages so low that our pay
Is never enough though we work all the day
When we ask for our money comes paper and string
Dear beef and bad mutton or some such like thing
Chor: *Derry down etc*

3. Bad weights and bad measures are frequently used
Oppressive extortion – so sorely abused;
Insulted and robbed too – we mention no names –
But pluck up our spirits and bowl in their frames
Chor: *Derry down etc*

4. Good people, oh pity our terrible case
Pray take no offence though we visit this place
We crave your assistance and pray for our foes
Oh may they find mercy when this life we lose
Chor: *Derry down etc*

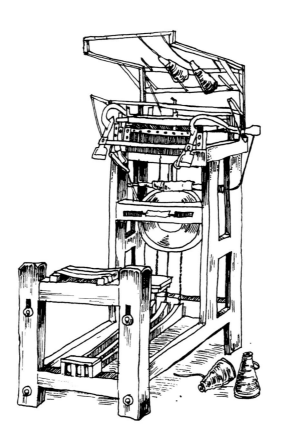

Poverty Knock

SAB

Trad. Tune from singing of Pete Coe
arr. Sally J Davies

Poverty Knock

Chorus
Poverty poverty knock,
My loom it is a-saying all day
O poverty poverty knock
Gaffer's too skinny to pay us
O poverty poverty knock
Keeping one eye on the clock
I know I can guttle
When I hear my shuttle
Go poverty poverty knock

1. Up ev'ry morning at five
   A wonder that we keep alive
   Tired and yawning
    In the cold morning
   And back to the dreary old drive

2. Oh dear, we're going to be late
   Gaffer is stood at the gate
   Our wages he'll docket
   We'll be out of pocket
   We'll have to buy grub on the slate
Chorus
(after every other verse)

3. Sometimes a shuttle flies out
   And gives some poor woman a clout
   There she lies bleeding
   With nobody heeding
   Oh who's going to carry her out?

4. The tuner should tackle my loom
   He'd rather sit on his bum
   And he's far too busy
   A-courting our Lizzie
   I just can't get him to come up
Chorus

5. Lizzie's so easily led
   I reckon he takes her to bed
   She always was skinny
   Now look at her pinny
   It's just about time they was wed

6. Oh dear, my poor head it sings
   I should have woven three strings
   The threads they keep breaking
   My poor heart is aching
   Oh God, how I wish I had wings
Chorus and coda

Tom of Bedlam

or

Mad Maudlin's Search for her Tom of Bedlam

SATB

Lyrics - Traditional
Tune - Dave Moran and Nic Jones
arr. Sally J Davies

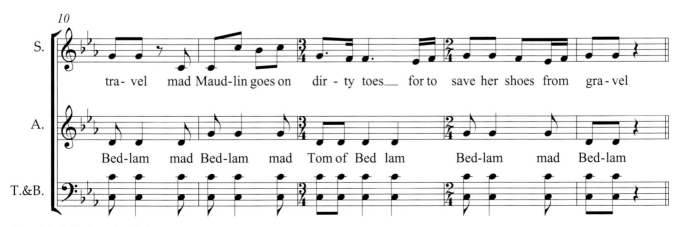

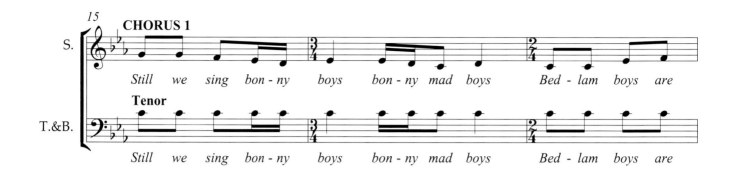

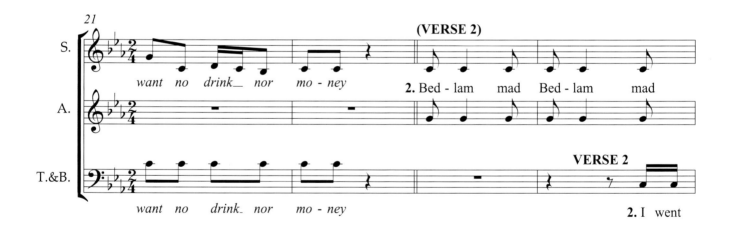

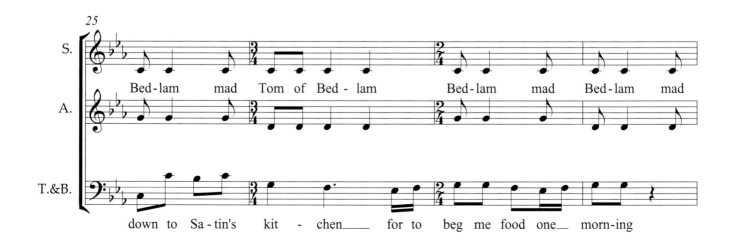

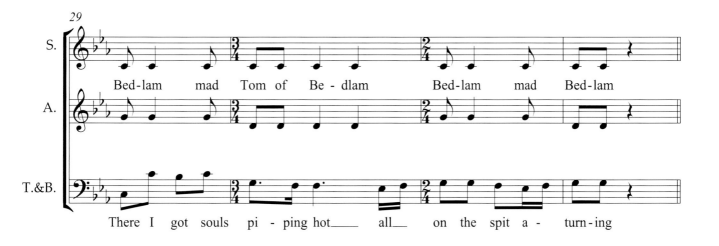

CHORUS 2

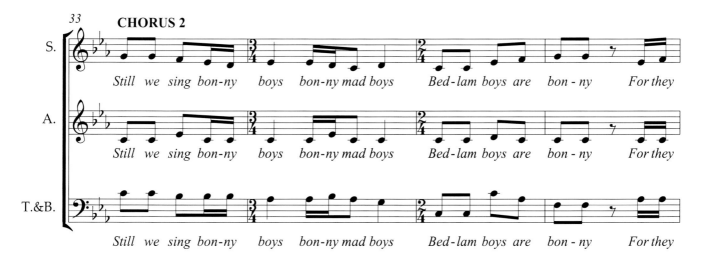

VERSE 5 & 6 (Altos - TUNE)

Tom of Bedlam

1. For to see mad Tom of Bedlam ten thousand miles I'd travel
Mad Maudlin goes on dirty toes for to save her shoes from gravel

Chorus
Still we sing bonny boys bonny mad boys
Bedlam boys are bonny
For they all go bare and they live by the air
And they want no drink nor money.

2. I went down to Satin's kitchen for to beg me food one morning
There I got souls piping hot all on the spit a-turning
Chorus *Still we sing bonny boys.....*

3. There I picked up a cauldron where boiled ten thousand harlots
Tho' full of flame I drank the same to the health of all such varlets
Chorus *Still we sing bonny boys.....*

4. My staff has murdered giants my bag a long knife carries
For to cut mince pies from children's thighs with which to feed the fairies
Chorus *Still we sing bonny boys.....*

5. The spirits white as lightning shall on my travels guide me
The moon would quake and the stars would shake whenever they espied me
Chorus *Still we sing bonny boys.....*

6. No gypsy slut nor doxy shall win my mad Tom from me
I'll weep all night the stars I'll fight the fray will well become me
Chorus *Still we sing bonny boys.....*

7. And when that I'll be murd'ring the man In the moon to a powder
His staff I'll break his dog I'll bake there'll howl no demon louder
Chorus *Still we sing bonny boys.....*

8. So drink to Tom of Bedlam he'll fill the seas in barrels
I'll drink it all well brewed with gall with mad Maudlin I will travel
Chorus *Still we sing bonny boys.....*

Tommy note

SATB

Broadside Ballad
Tune 'structured' by Jon Raven 1974
arr. Sally J Davies

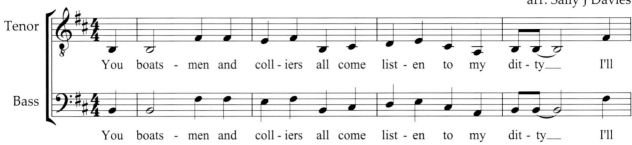

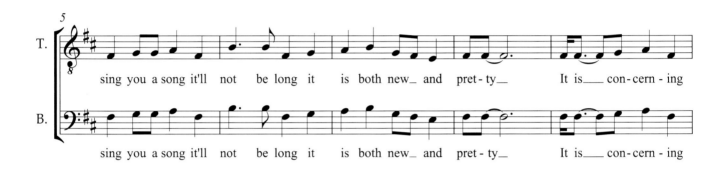

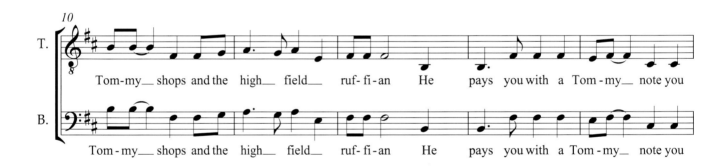

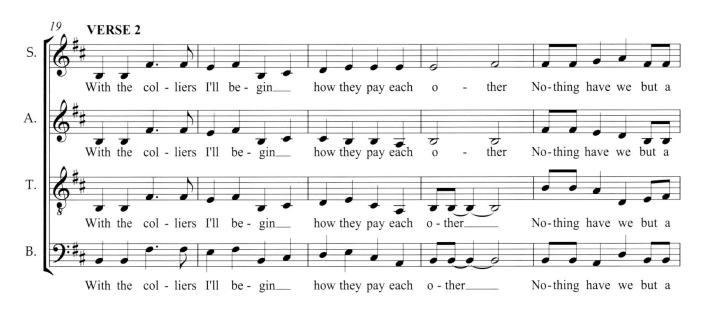

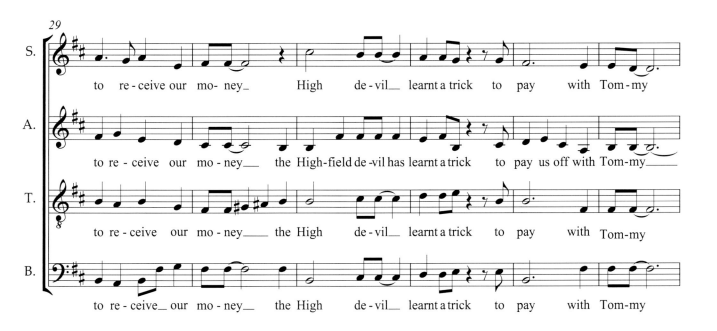

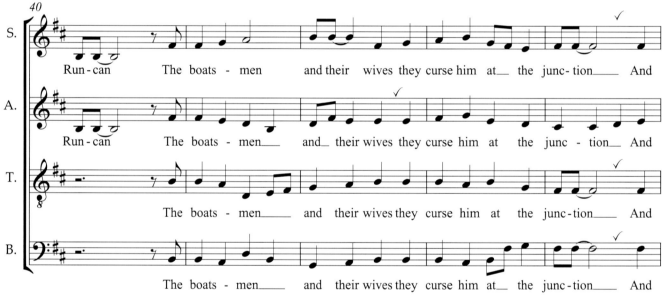

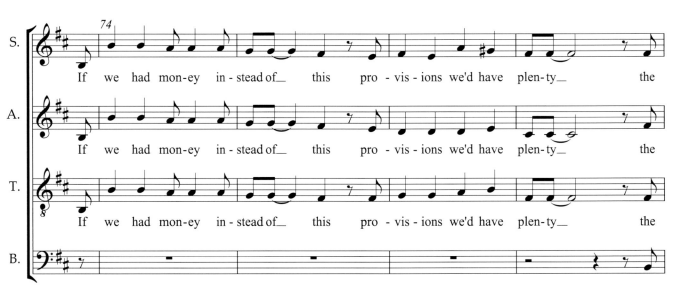

Tommy Note

1.   You boatsmen and colliers all come listen to my ditty
I'll sing you a song it'll not be long it is both new and pretty
It is concerning Tommy shops and the high field ruffian
He pays you with a Tommy note you must have that or nothing

2.   With the colliers I'll begin how they pay each other
Nothing have we but a Tommy note from one week to the other
On Saturday when a week's work is done and to receive our money
The High (field) devil has learnt a trick to pay (us off) with Tommy

3.   The boatsmen I now bring in that sails from Highfields to Runcan
The boatsmen and their wives they curse him at the junction
And all belonging to that branch that knows the art of boating
Wishing the tiller down his throat it would be a means to choke him

4.   When they have done their Runcan voyage and gone to collect their money
One half stops for hay and corn the other half for Tommy
Then to the Tommy Shop we go to fetch our week's provision
Our oatmeal sugar salt and soap scant weight and little measure

5.   If we had money instead of this provision we'd have plenty
The profit they get out of us it is nine shillings out of twenty
Come gear the horse and clear the line and jump on board the boat
Both night and day we'll steer away for another Tommy note

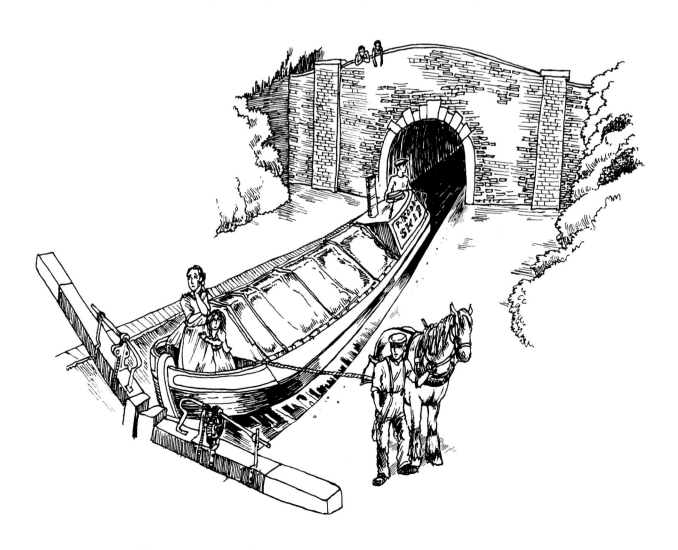

The Outlandish Knight

SATB

Traditional
arr. Sally J Davies

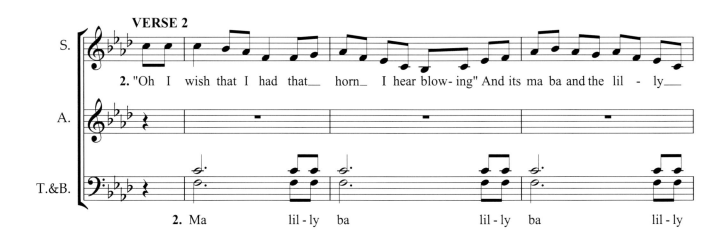

VERSES 4 and 5

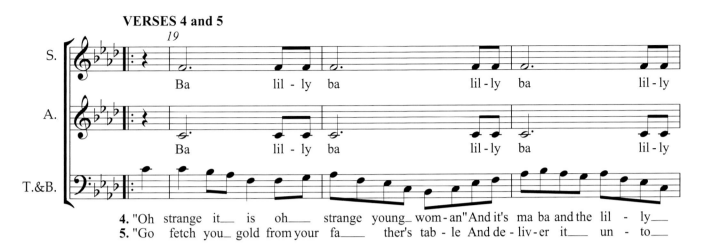

S. Ba lil - ly ba lil - ly ba lil - ly

A. Ba lil - ly ba lil - ly ba lil - ly

T.&B.
4. "Oh strange it__ is oh__ strange young__ wom - an" And it's ma ba and the lil - ly__
5. "Go fetch you__ gold from your fa__ ther's tab - le And de - liv - er it__ un - to__

S. ma ba lil - ly Ma__ On the / Where__

A. ma ba lil - ly Ma__ On the / Where__

T.&B.
ba "I can scarce blow my horn since I hear you a call-ing On the
me And the two fast-est hors - es in your fa-ther's sta-ble Where__

S. ve - ry first morn - ing of May' three"__
there__ stand thir - ty and

A. ve - ry first morn - ing of May" three"__
there__ stand thir - ty and

T.&B.
ve - ry first morn - ing of May" three"__
there__ stand thir - ty and

VERSES 6 and 10 (music as V1)

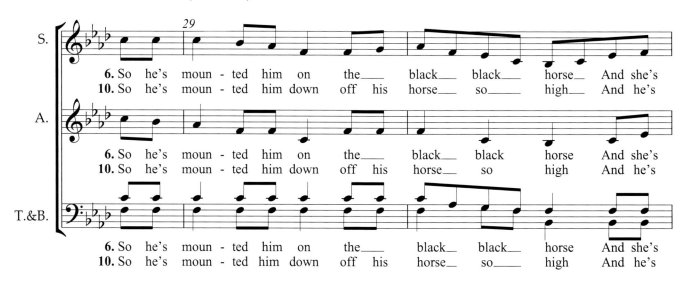

VERSES 7 and 8

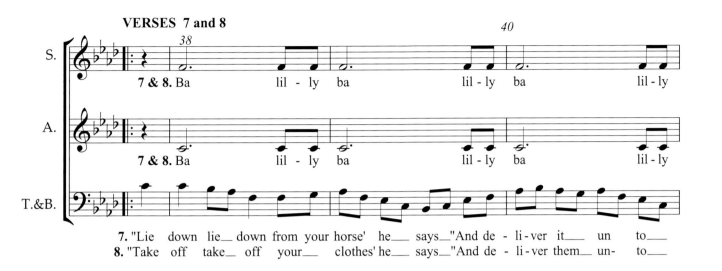

S. *38*
7 & 8. Ba   lil - ly ba   lil - ly ba   lil - ly

A.
7 & 8. Ba   lil - ly ba   lil - ly ba   lil - ly

T.&B.
7. "Lie down lie__ down from your horse' he__ says__"And de - li - ver it__ un to__
8. "Take off take__ off your__ clothes' he__ says__"And de - li - ver them__ un- to__

S. *41*
ma ba lil - ly   Ma_____   And the
For to

A.
ma ba lil - ly   Ma_____   And the
For to

T.&B.
me   For it's six   pret - ty maids I have drown-ed__ here And the
me   For__ they   are too fine and__ cost - ly__ robes For to

S. *44*
sev - enth one   you   shall   be | 1. sea" | 2.
rot__ in the   salt   salt

A.
sev - enth one   you   shall   be_____
rot__ in the   salt   salt   sea"_____

T.&B.
sev - enth one   you   shall__   be
rot__ in the   salt   salt__   sea"

The Outlandish Knight

1. Lady Margaret she sits in her bower sewing
Ma ba and the lilly ba
When she saw the knight with his horn a-blowing
On the very first morning of May

2. 'Oh I wish that I had that horn I hear blowing'
And it's ma ba and the lilly ba
'And that young knight to sleep here on my breast
On the very first morning of May'

3. Well the lady she had these words scarce spoke
And it's ma ba and the lilly ba
When in at her window the knight come a-jumping
On the very first morning of May

4. 'Oh strange it is oh strange young woman
And it's ma ba and the lilly ba
I can scarce blow my horn since I hear you a-calling
On the very first morning of May

5. 'Go fetch you gold from your father's table
And deliver it unto me
And the two fastest horses in your father's stable
Where there stand thirty and three'

6. 'So he's mounted him on the black black horse
And she's rode on the dappled grey
And they rode till they come to the broad sea shore
Just three hours before it was day

7. 'Lie down lie down from your horse' he says
'And deliver it unto me
For it's six pretty maids I have drownèd here
And the seventh one you shall be

8. 'Take off, take off your clothes,' he says
'And deliver them unto me
For they are too fine and costly robes
For to rot in the salt salt sea'

9. 'Lie down lie down from your horse' she says
'And turn your back on me
For it's not fitting that any gentle man
A naked lady should see'

10. So he's mounted him down off his horse so high
And he's turned his back on she
And she catched him around the middle so small
And tumbled him all down in the sea

11. Sometimes he sank, sometimes he swam
And it's ma ba and the lilly ba
'Oh help, oh help, oh my pretty mistress
Or drownèd I shall be'

12. 'Lie there, lie there oh you false young man
Lie there instead of me
For it's six pretty maids you have drownèd here
And the seventh one has drownèd thee'

CONTENTS, ALPHABETICAL